Farm
Facts

Plants
on the Farm

by Lisa J. Amstutz

raintree
a Capstone company — publishers for children

Raintree is an imprint of Capstone Global Library Limited, a company incorporated in England and Wales having its registered office at 264 Banbury Road, Oxford, OX2 7DY – Registered company number: 6695582

www.raintree.co.uk
myorders@raintree.co.uk

Edited by Jill Kalz
Picture research by Kelly Garvin
Originated by Capstone Global Library

Designed by Ashlee Suker
Production by Katy LaVigne
Printed and bound in India

ISBN 978 1 4747 6869 6 (hardback)   ISBN 978 1 4747 6885 6 (paperback)

British Library Cataloguing in Publication Data
A full catalogue record for this book is available from the British Library.

Acknowledgements
We would like to thank the following for permission to reproduce photographs: iStockphoto: Peopleimages, 5, xuanhuongho, 16-17; Shutterstock: Alexsander Dickov, 7, frank60, 8 (bottom), Gordon Bell, cover, Grandpa, backcover, 13, images72, 11, Jerry Hobert, 19, KucherAV, 6, MarcoFood, 14, mareandmare, 10, nawamin, 9 (top), oksana2010, 15, Ordinary On, 1, Peter Gudella, 3, PhotosOK, 22, slava17, 18, surachet khamsuk, 9 (bottom), V J Matthew, 12, Valentyn Volkov, 4, Visual Intermezzo, 8 (top), volodimir bazyuk, 20-21
Design Element:Shutterstock: Dudarev Mikhail, J.Schelkle, K.Narloch-Liberra, laura.h, Sichon
Every effort has been made to contact copyright holders of material reproduced in this book. Any omissions will be rectified in subsequent printings if notice is given to the publisher.

Contents

Growing crops

We use plants for many things.

Farmers grow plants to sell.

They call them crops.

Let's eat

Some farmers grow grains.
Wheat is a grain. The seeds
are crushed to make flour.
The flour is used to make
bread and cakes.

corn

Corn is a grain.

So is rice.

We eat the seeds.

Animals do too.

rice

corn field

rice field

Many fruits grow on trees. Farmers pick them when they are ready. Some fruits, such as bananas and oranges, grow in hot countries.

Potatoes grow underground. Their leaves and stems poke out of the soil. When the plants are fully grown, the farmer digs up the potatoes.

Pea plants grow very tall. They make pods. Can you count the peas inside this pod?

Farms around the world

Sugar cane is usually grown in hot countries. It is a tall grass. Sugar is made from sugar cane.

Cotton is grown in the United States, India and China. It grows around the seeds of cotton plants. It is used to make cloth.

Fields of sunflowers grow in France.

We use sunflower oil in cooking.

Glossary

cloth a material that is made from fibres such as cotton or wool; cloth is used to make clothing

crop a plant farmers grow in large amounts, usually for food

flour a powder made by crushing seeds of grains, such as wheat, corn, rye or oats

fruit the fleshy, juicy part of a plant that contains seeds and usually can be eaten

grain wheat or other type of grassy plant

pod case that grows around the seeds of the some plants

Find out more

Books

A Nature Walk on the Farm (Nature Walks), Louise and Richard Spilsbury (Raintree, 2015)

Learning About Plants (The Natural World), Catherine Veitch (Raintree, 2014)

The Farm (A Visit to), Blake Hoena (Raintree, 2019)

Websites

Find out about food and farming in the 5–8 years section:
www.foodafactoflife.org.uk

Watch a video of a working farm:
www.bbc.com/bitesize/clips/z9qtfg8

Comprehension questions

1. What part of the rice plant do we eat?

2. What kinds of things do you think could be made from cotton cloth?

3. What kind of crop would you like to grow and why?

Index